PREDATOR IN THE PULPIT

Predator In The Pulpit

Healing From Clergy Sexual Misconduct And Spiritual Abuse In The Church

NIKISHA SIMS

Warrior Princess Nation, LLC

Copyright © 2023 by Nikisha Sims

All rights reserved. No part of this book may be reproduced in any manner whatsoever without written permission except in the case of brief quotations embodied in critical articles and reviews.

First Printing, 2023

Published by
Warrior Princess Nation, LLC
6935 Aliante Pkwy Ste 104-423 North Las Vegas, NV 89084

Scriptures taken from the following

Stern, D. H. (1998). Complete Jewish Bible: an English version of the Tanakh (Old Testament) and B'rit Hadashah (New Testament) (1st ed., Mt 6:6–13). Jewish New Testament Publications.

Holy Bible, New Living Translation copyright © 1996, 2004, 2007 by Tyndale House Foundation. Used by permission of Tyndale House Publishers Inc., Carol Stream, IL 60188. All rights reserved. New Living, NLT, and the New Living Translation logo are registered trademarks of Tyndale House Publishers.

Scripture taken from *The Message*. Copyright © 1993, 1994, 1995, 1996, 2000, 2001, 2002. Used by permission of NavPress Publishing Group.

The Passion Translation (B. Simmons, trans.;). (2017). BroadStreet Publishing.

Scripture quotations marked TPT are from The Passion Translation®. Copyright © 2017, 2018, 2020 by Passion & Fire Ministries, Inc. Used by permission. All rights reserved. ThePassionTranslation.com.

"Scripture quotations taken from the Amplified® Bible (AMP), Copyright © 2015 by The Lockman Foundation. Used by permission. lockman.org"

CONTENTS

COPYRIGHT - iv
DEDICATION - viii

Introduction
1

Natural, Unnatural, And Supernatural
5

~ 1 ~
The Pulpit Predator
12

~ 2 ~
The Partner
21

~ 3 ~
The Process
27

vi ~ *Contents*

~ 4 ~

The Target

35

~ 5 ~

The Event

41

~ 6 ~

The Cycle

47

~ 7 ~

The Wounded

54

~ 8 ~

The Bystander

59

~ 9 ~

The Dragon

65

~ 10 ~

The Healer

72

~ 11 ~

The Pieces

84

Contents ~ vii

~ 12 ~

The Repair

89

~ 13 ~

The Resources

97

ABOUT THE AUTHOR - 100

To the hurting, who can't seem to see past the pain,
this is for you.
You are seen, you are heard, and you are loved.
It's time to heal!

To my husband, Randy, the bright light God used to
reveal the chaos and break the cycle.
Thank you for holding me on my darkest days. You
saw my brokenness and loved me anyway.

INTRODUCTION

We all experience life hurts. Painful situations we struggle to overcome and that define a season or multiple seasons in our lives. I have had my fair share; I'm sure you have too. Some are so painful that we can be reluctant to talk about or share them with others. Skeletons in the Closet is a term we have used to describe some of those painful and even shameful hurts. Tucking them away in the closet is not allowing us to heal. What happens if you take those hurts to a safe place to begin the healing process? You most likely will learn to move forward and live a healthier life. What happens if you take those situations to an unhealthy church? The place that is supposed to be safe but is not. By the way, unhealthy churches don't always look unhealthy on the surface. They could be growing in numbers and popularity, doing amazing things for the community, and still governed by unhealthy leadership. But what happens if your weaknesses and pain are exploited and manipulated for another individual's gain, satisfaction, and narcissistic tendencies, especially those in spiritual leadership authority? I'll tell you what happens; a festered, deep-seated hurt often called "church hurt."

Church hurt is real in that it is spiritual abuse, and it is more than unfortunate; it's life-shattering. People have taken their lives or had their lives destroyed because of it. Church hurt tears down the very institution that God created to lead the spiritually void and hurting to Himself that they may grow in community with one another. Church hurt does the exact opposite. It turns people away from God and the intimacy God desires to have with his people. The relationship that Jesus died to secure. The hurt is so deep that it is often kept in the dark recesses of hearts and never shared with another soul. The hurting goes around limping along, trying to make it through this life, wounded and afraid. After all, where do you go when the church hurts you?

I know what you're thinking, or at least what I was thinking. We should not go to church expecting people to solve our issues, the painful life situations we face, or our weaknesses in the first place. Shouldn't those be things that only God can deal with. Or maybe you think that the church is filled with broken people and that hurt people, hurt other people. People who are hurting indeed have the tendency to harm or lash out at other people. Still, I want us to look deeper, explore the dark pews, and stumble across a unique creature that lurks within the walls of our places of worship – The Predator in the Pulpit.

The Pulpit Predators, as I call them, are disguised as leaders of the people whom God has placed in their care. They look the part and play the role, but all along, seek the vulnerable, systematically weakening and tearing down their prey. Yes, prey. Just as a wild animal seeks out its prey in the wilderness, the Pulpit Predator seeks out its Target. It is systematic because it follows a pattern that can be duplicated and replicated. What makes it so painful is that it is often prolonged by others in leadership. They dismiss it, move the Pulpit Predator to another location where it is just repeated, or worse yet, they blame the Target for it happening in the first place. Clergy Sexual Misconduct, or CSM, is a real and prevalent problem in more churches than we care to know. A few well-broadcasted examples pale in comparison to the thousands of victims or Targets who remain silent every year. In these pages lay their voices, my voice, and may they both be heard loud and clear.

Targets are not always children. Children are easier for mankind to accept as "victims," but when the Target is an adult, they are no longer viewed in the same light. A slight difference exists between those who willfully seek to engage in adulteress relationships with people of power and those preyed upon by people in positions of power. We tend to lump them all in the same category. Adult Targets are just as vulnerable as children. They walk in various wounds, hurts, or weaknesses; they are blindsided by the unexpected and are guilted into silence, allowing the abuser, the Pulpit Predator, to continue the cycle of abuse.

Pulpit Predators are relentless in the process of grooming a Target, getting them ready, and steering them in the direction of the trap or event. If you are a Target, it is hard to recognize that it is a trap until it's too late. Most Targets blame themselves, thinking they caused the hideous acts somehow, and even more so if they stay and it continues to occur. As any person that remains in an abusive relationship, the Target feels obligated to stay, guilty for wanting to leave, or afraid to; all things they have been groomed to believe. How? Let's take a look at the grooming process and all that goes along with this form of abuse.

Understanding the psychology and how the Pulpit Predator operates allows us to recognize, expose, and disempower them. This is in the hopes that they seek wise and godly counsel that leads to true repentance and healing for the hundreds of thousands of Targets they have victimized.

NATURAL, UNNATURAL, AND SUPERNATURAL

In order for you to understand what you are about to read, it's essential for you to know a few things intentionally not covered in the introduction. So much of this book is from personal experience, as well as knowledge from research. I have, however, lived and recovered from the deep wounds of spiritual abuse. I refused to write a book from the place of pain, so I waited. I waited for God to heal the wounds of my heart. I waited until I self-healed in the context of therapy, both Christian and non-Christian. I waited until Holy Spirit said it was time. There is so much peace in writing; it's therapeutic. This is my continued therapy and my journey to help those who have been hurt in the safest place there is on earth; THE CHURCH! Not the building, because it is just that, a building without a soul, without life. I'm referring to the community of believers and followers of Yeshua the Messiah, also known as Jesus, the Christ, (you will read find me using either name), who weekly gather in a building that we call "church." But, just like the disciples in the New Testament and the patriarchs of the Old Testament, we are flawed individuals. We don't always walk according to the will of God for our lives. None of us do! Even Jesus said not to call him good, for only God is good. (Luke 18:19)

As you read, please reserve your judgment. Read with an open heart. Read with a desire to be informed, teach, and take action to heal the body of believers in your local community and in the global Church. I believe that is the purpose of my experience and my writing. I refuse to allow the Adversary to keep me silent and another person to have a similar experience. There have already been far too many, more than you can possibly imagine. For those of us who have had this personal experience, please don't condemn the Church over the actions of a few, and by all means, please don't hold God hostage with your pain. It's time to heal! You have carried the weight of silence, guilt, and shame for far too long. This book was mainly written for you. Yup, you! I want you to see yourself differently than how you may feel and how others may have labeled you. I want you to see yourself the way God sees you. Healed! Whole! Free!

There are some people that I want to introduce you to. While some of these characters are involved in all forms of abuse, for the purpose of this book, they are related to spiritual and sexual abuse. You will read more about them later, but I want to allow you time to see them. You need the time to know who you are about to face. Some of them will be easier to face than others. Whether or not church hurt is your personal experience, these characters will create a tidal wave of emotions. For some of them, you will have sympathy, and for others, pure hatred. Your emotions will all depend on your personal bias. Allow the emotions to flow. Cry, scream, or get angry if you must, but don't get stuck; release those emotions. Remember, this is about a process of healing, and healing never happens when we are stuck. Take a deep breath.

The Pulpit Predator

- It is at the hands of this individual, male or female, that seeks out, manipulates, and controls their Target. They are crucial in what I have labeled "The Event." The Pulpit Predator holds the position of power or authority within the church and within the event. They are respected in their position and often in the community. Pulpit Predators are arrogant and crafty in deception or well-covered in protection by those around them. Neither of which is beneficial for their Targets. They are educated, well-versed in the Scriptures, and excellent communicators. The hurt they inflict is never about sex but motivated by control or a self-inflated ego. You will read many details because I want you to see how they operate. Better said, I want you to see how the Dragon operates through them. I want you to be able to spot them so that you can protect others and even help the Pulpit Predator. Even they need healing.

The Partner

- This person assists the Pulpit Predator but is not always a willing participant and, therefore, not as easy to spot. If an unwilling participant, they have been blinded by the Pulpit Predator's manipulation. They overlook the red flags in an attempt to keep the peace or in good standing with the Pulpit Predator. If the Partner is a willing participant, they not only overlook red flags, they justify them. The Partner will blame someone else or believe it to be a one-time event, so neglect the need to deal with it. Willing Partners almost always protect the Pulpit Predator. They fail to protect the Target, giving the Pulpit Predator motivation to continue their abuse. The Partner can also be a fellow predator.

The Target

- This is just what it sounds like. The Target is the one that is pursued by the Pulpit Predator, either directly or indirectly. There is an entire process to this that you will read about. The Target will usually carry the guilt and shame of the event, blaming themselves entirely. Targets are not just children; they can also be adults. For this book, we will deal with adult Targets. They are the hardest to heal because they don't see themselves as victims or Targets because society has told them they can not be. If you are an adult, you are told that you played some role in the events. Targets do not willingly participate in abuse but are sought out by the Pulpit Predator and manipulated through a specific process.

The Wounded

- You may be wondering why the Target is not the Wounded. Yes, they carry wounds, but the Target is hunted, unlike the Wounded. The Wounded is hurt by proxy. They make up the local body of the church, where the Pulpit Predator is the leader. They are called the Wounded because they either split in their support of the Target or Pulpit Predator, or they literally split, forming another congregation. Their focus is drawn to the Event and away from God. For some, the event is enough for them to walk entirely away from God.

The Bystander

- Even after being a Target myself, this is the character my heart goes to the most. The Bystander is the one outside of the body of believers. They learn of the event from others, usually through gossip but sometimes through media, including social media. They can blame the global Church or even God if they have experienced their own trauma in the past. They are less likely to feel safe in the safest place in the world, and they are less likely to heal.

The Dragon

- Not much needs to be said here about this character. Ultimately, he is behind every event. I use the name Dragon because that is his depiction in the book of Revelation. He desires nothing more than to see events devour the Church. He can only be who he is; liar, devourer, thief, killer, destroyer, and enemy. We do ourselves a disservice by thinking and teaching that he has no power. When really he has some power here on earth allotted to him, he just doesn't have ALL power. Every ounce of manipulation stems from him; if our hearts are not guarded, he will use not only the Pulpit Predator but us as well.

The Healer

- There should be no need for an introduction here, but I can't assume everyone reading will know Him. The Healer is none other than Yahweh, God, our Heavenly Father. There is so much to be said about the Healer. He brings life to that which the Dragon destroys. For all the others that are damaged because of the event, He has the power to not only heal but to restore. He turns tragedies into triumphs and wounds into weapons. You and the lover of your soul collide. My heart is filled with anticipation, and I hope yours is as well, to see what the Healer will do by the end of this book.

"What sorrow awaits the leaders of my people—the shepherds of my sheep—for they have destroyed and scattered the very ones they were expected to care for," says the Lord. Therefore, this is what the Lord, the God of Israel, says to these shepherds: "Instead of caring for my flock and leading them to safety, you have deserted them and driven them to destruction. Now I will pour out judgment on you for the evil you have done to them." Jeremiah 23:1-2 NLT

~ 1 ~

THE PULPIT PREDATOR

The predator wants your silence. It feeds their power,
entitlement, and they want it to feed your shame.~
Viola Davis

Church leadership has always been a topic of conversation, whether negative or positive, since the early church. We view those in leadership as either inherently good and above others or devious, depending on our experience. Neither of which is totally accurate. While those in leadership positions have had issues, the need for such positions is as old as the church itself.

Church leaders have an array of titles depending on the sect or denomination. For the sake of this book, we will refer to the terms pastors and teachers. Pastors can also be teachers, but sometimes they are not and play different roles in leadership, such as overseers. In some congregations, only one pastor oversees the entire flock (congregation); in others, there can be multiple pastors who all perform different tasks. Regardless of the title, pastors are shepherds who have been given the ultimate assignment of caring for the flock. They also bear organizational leadership tasks like those found within a corporate structure.

Corporations have a hierarchy of leadership. The hierarchy can look different depending on the type of corporation, just as in the church. The hierarchy lends structure within that organization; without it, there would be misdirection and even chaos. The need for such hierarchy within the church is laid out in Scripture. In Colossians 1:18, Paul writes that "He" (The Messiah) is the head of the church. Paul goes on to say that he has become a servant to present the Word of God in its totality. He demonstrated biblical structure with Christ as the head and Paul as a servant leader. There were also other leaders who assisted Paul. Leadership within the church is not bad, and it is necessary.

Why all the background? Because it is essential to understand that the structure of the church's governing system and leadership was God's idea, not man's. Understanding this helps us isolate an individual from the corporate Church. One leader's misconduct doesn't represent the whole; however, there is an ever-growing cancer within the church, a Predator in the Pulpit.

A Pulpit Predator is someone who injures or exploits

others for personal gain or profit and, more than likely, is in a position of power. That power could be by physical brute force, abuse of authority, or psychological and emotional manipulation. More often than not, a Pulpit Predator's challenge is to gain control. This need to control may be for a variety of reasons, but it is what drives the behavior. Pulpit Predators could have, at some point, been Targets themselves and determined they would never be again. The control can be for financial gain, sexual activity, or even for notoriety. Whatever the reason, the results are the same: the injury and exploitation of another.

When Pulpit Predators gain control, they usually do anything to hang on to it. To lose control is a sign of defeat. They thrive in situations where they are in control, idolized, and sometimes worshipped. When that control is threatened, they will seek to destroy the threat. This destruction often paints the Target in a negative light, and the Pulpit Predator plays the role of the unappreciated victim. If confronted, denial or blame is the excuse they give with little to no genuine remorse. A Pulpit Predator is skilled in the art of grooming and can remain silent or dormant until they have mastered that art. There is a need to desensitize those around them so that predatory behavior is more acceptable or justified as playful, harmless, or overly affectionate and caring. Pulpit Predators use their spiritual authority to exploit those in their congregation for personal gain. This abuse of power is called spiritual abuse.

Not all Pulpit Predators are alike, but the process is. There are some female Pulpit Predators, but the majority are men. I believe this is because there are still congregations or denominations that will not allow women to take on leadership or pastoral roles; however, that is not the discussion of this book. Pulpit Predators in the church can come from any denomination or congregation size. Ethnic backgrounds vary as well as popularity and wealth. Regardless of the differences between a Pulpit Predator or the nature of personal gain or profit, it is always a moral failure. The most popular or televised moral failures in the church are sexual immorality and mismanagement of finances. In all actuality, the real moral failure is pride.

First pride, then the crash— the bigger the ego, the harder the fall. Proverbs 16:18 The Message

The well-known Pulpit Predators are seen in the news, and the church they oversee suffers a massive shakeup. But most likely, a Pulpit Predator's activities are never publicly exposed. The biggest problem is that those in smaller congregations think this predatory behavior only happens in mega-churches. Wrong! Believe it or not, hiding in a smaller congregation are lesser-known Pulpit Predators. The eyes of the world are not on them, and it can be easier to deceive, manipulate, and control the narrative of a smaller group. I have attended churches of various sizes and witnessed some form of abuse of power in the larger and smaller ones. Don't get caught up in what you see publicly; focus on the behavior or patterns of behaviors. Pulpit Predators are well-versed in God's word and often in psychology, formal or informal. They use the pulpit to maintain control over the Target and can even have multiple Targets active in the same congregation. They will use church work as an excuse to prey on and isolate Targets. Humility is often publicly displayed, while arrogance and manipulation are at the fabric of their being.

> *If you are wise and understand God's ways, prove it by living an honorable life, doing good works with the humility that comes from wisdom. But if you are bitterly jealous and there is selfish ambition in your heart, don't cover up the truth with boasting and lying. For jealousy and selfishness are not God's kind of wisdom. Such things are earthly, unspiritual, and demonic. For wherever there is jealousy and selfish ambition, there you will find disorder and evil of every kind.* **James 3:13-16 NLT**

A Pulpit Predator who abuses power for sex is just like any other sexual predator. The act of sex is coupled with their lust for control. The longer a Pulpit Predator gets away with their crime, their ego craves even more sex and power. I say crime because if the Pulpit Predator were in any other profession, like a teacher, therapist, or doctor, it would be punishable by the law. Instead, if a Pulpit Predator is exposed, they are allowed to "repent," and all is well again. This disregards the Target and sets the Pulpit Predator up to repeat the behavior. While the Pulpit Predator I encountered was not televised, their predatory behavior was known and covered up. Something I was not aware of until long after the abuse. He was allowed to move from one location to another, facing no criminal charges or repercussions from the church. The shame of it is that I was not his first Target. A Pulpit Predator will insist that his "moment of weakness" is a one-time occurrence. Their pridefulness may even have them boasting about having many women "before" they became pastors, but predatory behavior is learned behavior. It takes time to master the grooming pattern, so lying about the timeline of other Targets is no surprise.

What may be surprising to you is that writing the name of the Pulpit Predator I encountered in this book means I could be sued for slander and defamation of character. It happens to Targets all the time, which is why they remain silent. There are times when Targets are paid off to stay silent. There is a hole in the spiritual system that protects the Pulpit Predator. Where is the #metoo movement within the congregation? It's hidden behind a doctrine of grace. The Pulpit Predator teaches the doctrine of grace in a community church to justify their behavior, but there is no true love behind it. Pulpit Predators rarely take personal responsibility publicly. Their idea of grace is assuring the Target that God will not be angry at them or the Pulpit Predator because of God's great grace. The Pulpit Predators' inclusion of the Target as the object of anger is manipulative. It's designed to get the abused to take the abuser's responsibility for the event. They abuse such grace just as they abuse their spiritual authority, and there is no true repentance because the behavior continues either with the same Target or with a new one. While I believe God extends His grace towards us, the Pulpit Predator creates a church culture of abuse when they manipulate grace for the justification of sin and personal gain.

No matter your abusive encounter with a Pulpit Predator, you survived. I want to acknowledge that because sometimes the effects of abuse linger, and you may feel defeated. But you are stronger than you know. Be determined to live after abuse. So many allow the pain and sorrow to overwhelm them, taking their own lives. You made it through one of the most challenging chapters in this book, which is why I placed it near the top. I promise it gets easier after this, but I need to ask you for a favor before we get there. This will not be easy. No, I'm not going to ask you to forgive, at least not right now. Forgiving is something you must do at your own time and pace.

I will ask you to acknowledge. Acknowledge that the abuse took place and the pain it caused you. Acknowledge your anger. Write the Pulpit Predator a letter and destroy it if you choose. I wrote a letter to the Pulpit Predator I encountered as well as to his Partner and his spouse. AND I sent each one all three. No, you don't have to go that far for acknowledgment, but for my journey, I did. And you're probably guessing what happened. Nothing would be a correct answer; not one of them responded or acknowledged anything unless removing me as a friend on social media counts.

Nevertheless, I didn't send it to them for them, but for me. I needed to take back what I had been robbed of...power—the power to trust my judgment. Power to let go, to forgive, to trust, to love, and to give back the responsibility of his actions to the rightful owner, him. So acknowledge and take back what belongs to you and give up what doesn't. Also, never claim that person as yours. He is and never will be MY predator. He is simply a Pulpit Predator that I encountered. Begin to reclaim you. Just like this chapter, that horrible chapter in your life is ending. I speak that over you because I know it to be true. It's the purpose for which I am writing, to help you put a period where a comma had remained. Please take a deep breath; you can do it.

To those who know a Pulpit Predator or one of their Targets, now is your time for acknowledgment. Acknowledge that abuse has gone on too long. Don't stay silent. Determine to be part of the solution and healing process. A Pulpit Predator rarely acts alone. They often have Partners who do so willingly or out of ignorance. Partners are usually silent, never acknowledging the abuse.

But Peter and the apostles replied, "We must obey God rather than any human authority. Acts 5:29 NLT

~ 2 ~

THE PARTNER

Almost all Pulpit Predators have Partners. Partners assist the Pulpit Predator in the grooming process, whether they realize it or not. They are the ones that identify the weak points in the Target that can be exploited. Unfortunately, many engage in the process so much they have come to justify their behavior and that of the Pulpit Predator. Partners who dismiss and justify behavior may do so because the Pulpit Predator disillusions them.

A Partner's role is to befriend a Target, often at the request of a Pulpit Predator, and report back to the Pulpit Predator what they know about the Target. This is not usually so black and white. In the church community, parishioners befriend one another as they should. We were created to do life together. So, the relationship between a Partner and a Target can be genuine. Unfortunately, the Pulpit Predator finds an opportunity to use that relationship to gain closer access to the Target. They resort to persuasive or compassionate tactics like asking seemingly innocent questions or pretending they are concerned and would like to understand better how to pray for the Target. However, the most significant source of transference of information is gossip. Church gossip is like cancer, eating away and destroying the vital parts of God's community.

Partners have gone through their own grooming process. They are not being groomed to be Targets, but they are groomed to be silent or turn a blind eye. The predator's jokes and intentionally playful nature desensitize the Partner to problematic behavior. A culture is created, and Partners find the request of Pulpit Predators more and more difficult to resist. Even when they know of predatory behavior, they rarely report it and will side with the Pulpit Predator against the Target.

When I could finally discuss what was happening, I turned to a church friend. I thought it would be a safe place to figure things out. I was vulnerable, ashamed, embarrassed, and confused. The response I got from this fellow believer was nothing short of a slap in the face. I was told I was stupid for allowing it to happen because, after all, men will be men. I don't believe this Partner was heartless, although it felt like it at the time; I do know that when a predatory culture is created in the church, the primary task of that church is no longer the proclamation of Jesus but the protection of the Pulpit Predator.

A Partner can be the spouse of the Pulpit Predator, the

church assistant, or any other leader. They will usually have some form of authority themselves, although much less than the Pulpit Predator.

Spouses can be silent Partners. They can know of past Targets and blame them for any events that have taken place. At times, they carry an accusatory demeanor toward the Target even if the grooming of the Target has only just begun. A spouse may not know why they feel that way, but the Pulpit Predators will keep discord between the spouse and the Target. This happens when an escape route is being created. An escape route is a plan in which the spouse, persuaded by the Pulpit Predator, sees the Target as a threat. This allows the Pulpit Predator to easily play the victim role when confronted by the spouse after an event. For example, accusing the Target of seduction and thus labeling the event as an affair in which they had a "moment of weakness" or "lapse in judgment," something they claim was a one-time event and would never occur again.

Even with multiple Targets over the years, Pulpit Predators still convince the spouse to believe they would destroy the church if they sought a divorce, guilting them into staying in a marriage. This form of manipulation is just like any other form of spousal abuse. If the spouse encounters the same"men will be men" advice, they will remain in that abusive relationship no matter how miserable.

Unfortunately, there is the spouse who is the willing Partner. They know about Targets well in advance and choose to turn their heads. As long as the Pulpit Predator comes home, they justify the behavior as ok, and it's just the way it is. This spouse may have been a previous Target that married their Pulpit Predator or a woman the Pulpit Predator divorced his previous spouse to marry. There are times when the spouse is also a Pulpit Predator with their own Targets, and the marriage has a mutual understanding. Either way, the spouse that remains and the one who turns their head both play the role of the devoted spouse in the public eye.

Church assistants can be groomed into being Partners or becoming Targets themselves. Most of their time is spent with the Pulpit Predator, and a bond occurs. This bond ensures loyalty to the Pulpit Predator, especially if the Pulpit Predator has never been inappropriate with the assistant or the assistant is advanced in age. If the assistant was a previous Target, they are less likely to reveal the inappropriate behavior of the Pulpit Predator even if they recognize the pattern for two reasons. 1) They have mislabeled the event as an affair and fear isolation. 2) They feel intimidated and fear exposure. Guilt and shame are at the forefront of every Target remaining silent. Either way, the assistant justifies predatory behavior, dismissing it as joking, a one-time thing, or, even worse, not their business to intervene.

Unwilling Partners are controlled just as much as

Targets. It can be uncomfortable to confront the one in authority for fear of losing their job, being labeled by others as being too uptight or pious, causing chaos in the church, or ending a marriage. However, as Elie Wiesel points out, "We must take sides. Neutrality helps the oppressor, never the victim. Silence encourages the tormentor, never the tormented." It is never easy to take a stand for what you know to be right. If every Partner keeps silent, then every Pulpit Predator is allowed to roam freely from one Target to another. That's why this book is so important to me. Although once a Target, I refuse to sit back and become a Partner. My pain will be another person's victory, and my voice will break another person's silence.

Temptation comes from our own desires, which entice us and drag us away. These desires give birth to sinful actions. And when sin is allowed to grow, it gives birth to death. James 1:14-15 NLT

~ 3 ~

THE PROCESS

Grooming is more of a psychological process than any-thing else. It involves numerous steps that are meticu-lously planned and implemented. Depending on the Pulpit Predator and the Target, this process can take weeks, months, or years. This process aims to find the weakness in the Target that may be exploited. It's about gaining trust and loyalty and disarming the Target's senses. Red flags usually become less potent until they are accepted as normal behavior. No part of psychological manipulation is normal.

Grooming is used to herd the Target in the direction the Pulpit Predator desires. No Target willingly enters a situation where they are manipulated, controlled, and abused. Manipulation is the underlying fuel to the groom-ing process and is used to maintain control over the Target. It happens when there is an imbalance of power, and that power is used for selfish gain. Pulpit Predators also use spiritual manipulation. Manipulation usually isn't visible until the event is well over and the Target has entered the healing process. Even then, it will be hard for the Target to identify the manipulation.

In the grooming process, there are distinct stages. Again, this process is gradual, and these stages can take any length of time. Some stages are more progressive, so there is no time frame per stage. A Pulpit Predator can move within stages, meaning they may move to the next stage or repeat a stage. Maintaining control in each stage is essential.

There are six dominant stages.

• Select A Target

Selecting a Target is first on the list. This selection stage can be days, weeks, months, and even years. The Pulpit Predator will take time to select a Target with an apparent weakness that can be exploited. This could be anything from rejection, divorce, or grief. For me, it was divorce, an illness, and a child struggling with mental health. The Pulpit Predator is not as concerned with the cause of the weakness, only its impact on the Target's life. The greater the impact, the more susceptible the Target is to manipulation and oppression. I didn't realize at the time that I had been selected as a Target years before the grooming process took place. There were always inappropriate comments disguised as jokes. A Pulpit Predator will wait until they grow tired of other Targets or when the weakness of a desired Target is revealed. Weaknesses are often heart wounds. Heart wounds make it difficult for the Target to identify that they are prey. Even when I was told, "I'll pray for you, and that's p.r.e.y." I didn't recognize it as predatory behavior because no one wants to believe their pastor is a Pulpit Predator. And if he was a Pulpit Predator, surely someone would have stopped him from becoming or remaining a pastor. Once a Target is selected, the rest of the grooming process can occur.

• Gaining Trust

This stage is relatively simple for a Pulpit Predator. By definition, the job requires that trust be established. Just like a psychologist gains a patient's trust, the Pulpit Predator acts as a counselor, gaining the trust of parishioners. From relational to spiritual counseling, trust is foundational. In the process of grooming, it is mandatory. What were once red flags the Target would have recognized and confronted are now dismissed because established trust will cause a Target to second guess themselves.

• Filling A Need

Every weakness creates a need. It's a problem that needs a resolution, even when it's emotional. Pulpit Predators will either secretly or publicly meet the needs of the Target. If it is a physical need, the Pulpit Predator will purchase it, take it from church funds, or take up a collection.

No matter how the need is met, a Pulpit Predator will take responsibility for meeting it, thus securing a deeper level of trust. Even filling a need is manipulative, as the Target feels obligated and indebted. After a divorce and a new illness, I was without a job, on public assistance, and my car had been repossessed. I was secretly given a car by the Pulpit Predator and told not to tell anyone. What should have been a blessing turned into something entirely different. An obligation to be where he wanted me to be.

- Isolating the Target

To maintain trust and dependency and to manipulate the Target, a Pulpit Predator will go all out to isolate the Target. Pulpit Predators must keep their Targets away from others who would identify the red flags and expose the manipulation. When Pulpit Predators can't fully isolate the Target, they will solicit the help of Partners. As you know, Partners can be willing or unwilling participants. However, they will report the Target's activities to the Pulpit Predator. Since Partners can be unwilling, they may not know they are being used to monitor the Target's whereabouts, emotions, and interactions with others outside the Pulpit Predator's core group. Pulpit Predators will often ask Partners how the Target is doing out of "concern" for the Target. Getting as much information as they need to keep the manipulation going. The Partner must gain the Target's trust for this to be effective.

- The Event

The event is so important that it has a section on its own. However, I will state here that the event does not have to be a one-time thing; it can occur for months or years and reduces the self-esteem of the Target every time it occurs. For me, it was years. One form of manipulation used in the process is fear. The event amplifies that fear. Fear of discovery, fear of rejection, fear of God's anger, and fear of the Pulpit Predator are just some forms of fear. For the sake of this writing, the event is sexual contact. This contact can be inappropriate touching, kissing, oral, anal, vaginal intercourse, or any combination. It is not suggested or initiated by the Target. It is NOT consensual but coercive, and as stated by Chris Hansen, "It's not entrapment. Because the decoys never make the first move. Nor do they raise the issue of having sex. It's always the potential predator that does that.[1]" Manipulation and control make up the event's foundation, not love or intimacy, even when the Pulpit Predator or Target says I love you. The event can and will be labeled by the Pulpit Predator and others, often as an affair, but in this situation, it is abuse. Labeling it any other way places the responsibility of the event on the Target.

• Maintaining Control

Once the initial event has occurred, the Pulpit Predator rarely walks away from predatory behavior. They will attempt to maintain control to ensure reoccurring events or protect themselves from exposure. To maintain control, they will use blame and power shifting. The Pulpit

Predator will assume the role of the victim by insisting they are powerless and that the Target is in control. Stating things like they couldn't help themselves because of the Target's beauty, body, sexuality, or spirituality, also stating that the Target can destroy them, the Wounded (church), and the Bystander (unchurched) if the Target reveals the event. I heard it all. The purpose is to get the Target to take responsibility for the process and the event. The Pulpit Predator will not take responsibility even if they tell the Target they will. Even admitting to the Target that they are responsible is a form of emotional and mental abuse. They would never admit it publicly unless exposed; even then, it's a big if. Spiritual abuse is when the Pulpit Predator uses the Bible to maintain control. Giving sermons on what the Pulpit Predator was actively doing, as he called it, "sin," or that "someone" in the church had the power to destroy the church and must be mindful of their words and actions. Yes, I was the "someone" being referred to.

Psychological manipulation is not new. According to King Solomon, nothing under Heaven ever is. Solomon would have first-hand experience with this. His parent's relationship was a product of this form of manipulation. While we all admire King David, who is described as a man after God's heart, he had flaws. The difference between King David and the Pulpit Predator is that David was repentant. The Pulpit Predator seeks to repeat the process as many times as they can get away with.

[1] To Catch A Predator, Dateline NBC

Finally, grow powerful in union with the Lord, in union with his mighty strength. Ephesians 6:10 CJB

~ 4 ~

THE TARGET

Why the word Target? I chose the word Target because being a victim was harder for me to identify with as an adult. I carried full responsibility for the Pulpit Predator's actions on my shoulders because I didn't see myself as a victim. The negative connotation of the word was torturous for me to accept. Target, I understood. After all, I had been targeted. The word victim declared my identity, whereas Target identified the situation.

Targets have known and unknown weaknesses, making them vulnerable and susceptive to the grooming process. When I say weaknesses, I am speaking of emotional pain and blind spots. There is no age range or specific characteristics of a Target; it solely depends on a Pulpit Predator's desires. What all Targets have in common is they will, at some point, blame themselves for the event or define it as an affair of their own doing. Remember, not all sexual events are about sex but about power and control.

Some Targets have been involved in abusive situations with scars that have not yet been processed or healed, allowing predatory behavior to appear normal. There is such a thing as addiction to abuse, yet the Target is not to blame.

Targets can be preyed upon for years before they enter the grooming process. This preying does not end in the grooming process or after the event; it only intensifies. Targets fear shame and seek to avoid it by remaining silent, which is easier to do. In addition, Targets can battle depression, anxiety, and low self-esteem after the event, isolating themselves from the family and friends that could help them escape the abuse. The Partner became my closest friend, and my family, distant relatives.

Targets rarely identify as victims of abuse but often identify as being stupid and weak, which can be perpetuated by the Partner or Pulpit Predator. Targets are indeed victimized by abuse. It is never ok for clergy to engage in Clergy Sexual Misconduct with any congregant. Rev. Joel A. Bowman says, "For ministers of the Gospel to engage in sexual activity with members of their faith community, to whom they are not married, is exploitive and abusive of such persons...In the case of doctors or therapists, they could lose their license to practice if allegations of abuse were substantiated. Whether forced or "consensual," clergy sexual abuse is dead wrong, sinful, and yes, criminal." CRIMINAL! You read that right. What Targets experience is a criminal offense; however, not everyone identifies it as such.

At the time of this writing, according to Baylor University, there are 13 states: Arkansas, Connecticut, Delaware, Iowa, Kansas, Minnesota, Mississippi, New Mexico, North Dakota, Texas, South Dakota, Utah, Wisconsin, and the District of Columbia, that have criminal codes for clergy sexual relations with a congregant. The content of those codes often stated that consent by the complainant is no defense. Clergy have the same fiduciary responsibility to "do no harm" as the licensed therapist, doctor, or social worker would have due to the role of a counselor by the nature of their profession. While civil cases are often won, criminal cases are rarely pursued. Why? The First Amendment of the U.S. Constitution is often mentioned regarding freedom of speech, but it also has what is known as Establishment and Free Exercise clauses. I'm no law expert, but in short layman's terms, courts are limited in their authority to preside over cases of religion or enact laws that single out religion. So those 13 states and D.C. require clergy to be mandated reporters and opened the pathway for civil suits by extending the statute of limitations, or at least that's how most of the laws are interpreted. Criminal justice is rarely seen, civil suits can be undisclosed, and mandated reporting only works if the clergy is not the Pulpit Predator.

I know all of that can be discouraging, but it doesn't change the facts. A Target never chooses to be a Target and must accept that they were abused. Yes, adult Targets can be and are abused. What has happened to Targets is not what they sought out. The intent of the heart determines the motive of the action. I never intended for my life to be turned upside down. Going through a divorce, my daughter's crisis, and me suffering an illness was bad enough; add becoming someone's Target, and well, that nearly sent me over the edge. Depression set in, and although I smiled and acted as if nothing was wrong, I was tormented. I felt alone and isolated, embarrassed and ashamed. There were days I just wanted to end it. What kept me alive was I knew my daughter needed her mom. I fought for her mental health and mine. To say it was a difficult season is an understatement. Even as I write this, tears flow down my face, washing away the residue. Writing is therapeutic, so this is my therapy session. This is my fight for your mental health, your therapy, and your healing. I want you to know that you are heard, seen, and greatly loved.

After reading this, you may identify as a Target, but you don't have to remain one. For far too long, you have been blaming yourself for the events that have occurred. STOP! Determine in your heart that you will no longer allow an event or season of events to continue to control your life. It may be challenging to deal with church hurt and abuse, but it is not impossible. I do want you to know this, whatever has happened, it is no reflection of who God is or His love for you. Hearing that may not be easy to swallow right now, or maybe you clearly understand that.

Wherever you are on the spectrum of this difficult journey is ok for now, but movement is necessary for reaching the goal of healing and victory.

We must move in order to be free. If you are stuck or unwilling to move, you will miss out on the beauty that your future holds. Being a Target is not your life; it is definitely not the life God intended for you to have. For years, I was stuck in the role of a Target. I believed that if it was repeatedly happening, then I was to blame, so I pulled away from my God purpose and even from God. Hurting has that effect on us. The very thing we need the most in times like these we pull away from. God, family, and community will help you get unstuck and on the path to healing. Reaching out is not easy; I know firsthand what it's like. Scary! Having to reveal what you are most ashamed of will never be easy, at least not at first. Here's the deal: being stuck is the very plan of the enemy of your soul, Satan, or whom I call the Dragon.

I was buried in guilt and shame and, for years, stuck. I refused to do anything I knew God had called me to do. The pain was so deep I felt as if I was unforgivable and that I had blown the calling of God on my life. Whenever I made any effort to walk in my calling, it seemed pointless and ineffective. And the Pulpit Predator made sure he was even in control of that. The Dragon constantly resurfaced the events and reminded me of my shame, guilt, feelings of unworthiness, and a whole list of other lies. I resolved that I would never minister, speak, mentor, or ever write again. I boxed God into my world of never as if His power was limited by my pain or by the words of the Dragon. You are reading this because the Healer's power is greater than anything I have faced or will face. His power is greater than your circumstances and your pain as well.

Healing is a process. Please don't allow anyone to tell you any different. You will have moments of triumph and those in which you feel like you are starting from ground zero. In the healing process, God will reveal your weaknesses and strengths to better equip you for the next challenging situation. Yes, there will be other difficult life situations, and while they may not be as extreme as what has happened to you now, difficulties will come. However, you are strong enough to survive this. You will make it through the healing process. You will thrive. You will reclaim your life, and your story will be that of victory. Don't quit!

~ 5 ~

THE EVENT

The event is any and every situation that is manipulative and coercive with an intentional design to gain control over the Target for personal advancement or satisfaction. I know that was a mouthful. In essence, the event can occur at any place and at any time for the benefit of the Pulpit Predator. The Pulpit Predator calculates the event well in advance and will often steer the Target toward a path leading to the event. Like scheduling meetings and then telling everyone else that the meeting is canceled except for the Target, as was in my experience. The idea is to isolate the Target to make it harder to resist or escape.

The details of an event are different depending on the Pulpit Predator, but they always follow a specific pattern. Remember that meeting I said was scheduled? That was steering me in the direction that the Pulpit Predator desired. Yes, I should have had discernment, but because

I was not anticipating what would happen next, my guard was down. The grooming process had been effective. Once in the office, yes, the church office, he locked the door, and everything in me then began to scream. I had been sexually assaulted before, and that same sickening feeling was rising up; although I was trying to keep calm, I was starting to panic. I was alone in a converted warehouse on a less frequented street. I simply said I needed to leave. I was backed into a wall, kissed, then instructed to sit, and he completely undressed, and that is when I knew my worst nightmare was about to take place....again. His only words to me were, "I have waited a long time for this." When it was over, I laid at the altar and wept. The only place I knew to turn was to God, and I needed to gather myself before I faced my family. Even that moment was interrupted by the lie that he would take full responsibility and that God was not angry with me. Classic grooming tactic. The next day, he purchased the morning-after pill. His comment, "God told me you were fertile." I took the pill.

That event created a lot of fear in me. Everything about me changed, and I tried desperately to hide it because of the guilt and shame I felt. I took total responsibility for the event, especially when it happened again. By that point, I had shut down and began to get increasingly ill, and the manipulation, coercion, and threats continued. I began to play a role I hated, depression set in, events continued to happen, and I wanted to end my own life, especially when I became pregnant. Why didn't I tell anyone? I did. The

PREDATOR IN THE PULPIT ~ 43

Partner I thought I could trust, but I was shamed, and he was excused as just being a man. So, the isolation from family and friends increased, and so did the manipulation. He told me I would destroy the church if I didn't get an abortion. He told me that he had a tie around his neck and would kill himself, and only I could prevent it. Then, the messages from the pulpit began to reference how people and the decisions they made could destroy the church. That wasn't the only message from the pulpit. The stress was unbelievable, and on Good Friday, I sat in the pew of a large church and had a miscarriage with a smile on my face and pain in my heart without one person knowing what I was going through. Silence is deadly.

I could keep going, but I don't want to make this solely about my personal experience. You have your own experience or know someone who does. Every event is traumatic, and every Target responds differently. Please don't call yourself or that person weak, stupid, or any other non-supportive derogatory term. They have already done enough of that on their own. As I sit writing this, I have paused along the way to weep over the events I experienced and over yours. Again, writing is therapeutic, and even though I have had a lot of therapy, there is still an emotional release as I write and share my story. It may be the same for you, but you are not alone. Even an entire congregation can be a Target.

If the entire congregation is the Target, then the Pulpit Predator will present, in public, a need so great and urgent that it makes it hard for the congregation to resist. Now, there are serious needs in our world and situations where the need for churches to act is urgent, beneficial, or an act of worship.

And all the believers met together in one place and shared everything they had. They sold their property and possessions and shared the money with those in need. They worshiped together at the Temple each day, met in homes for the Lord's Supper, and shared their meals with great joy and generosity—all the while praising God and enjoying the goodwill of all the people. And each day the Lord added to their fellowship those who were being saved. Acts 2:44-47 NLT

The motive behind the need is not always honorable and should be evaluated. One way to evaluate is to see how the funds are being used. Whatever the urgent need, there should be a positive impact by the congregation's actions. Even when giving to leadership for their work in the ministry, which is important, it should come from a desire of the congregation, not coercion.

You Philippians well know, and you can be sure I'll never forget it, that when I first left Macedonia province, venturing out with the Message, not one church helped out in the give-and-take of this work except you. You were the only one. Even while I was in Thessalonica, you helped out—and not only once, but twice. Not that I'm looking for handouts, but I do want you to experience the blessing that issues from generosity. **Philippians 4:15-17 The Message**

To reiterate, not all events are sexual, but all events are about power. Events can be reoccurring or isolated. The true nature will always be masked in secrecy and deception. The setting up of an event will be at the hand of the Pulpit Predator and sometimes the Partner. The Target nor the Wounded will ever initiate the event. This is what makes it spiritual and sexual abuse by definition.

Excuses can be used to recreate an event at a moment's notice. Isolated events are devastating but often can yield a faster healing process. Reoccurring events can push a Target into hopelessness, a feeling of helplessness, depression, further isolation, and almost always shame and guilt, delaying the healing process. Delayed healing makes it more difficult for the Target to forgive, and unforgiveness breeds bitterness. To quote author Alan Paton, "When a deep injury is done us, we never recover until we forgive." Bitterness, as with guilt and shame, holds the Target bound to the experience, not allowing them to move forward, leaving the door open for the event to reoccur. As in any abusive relationship, recurring events can carry on for months or years. Every time an event happens, it becomes easier for the next event to occur.

Again, Targets do not create events and do not ask for events to reoccur. When Targets attempt to escape or prevent reoccurring events, the Pulpit Predator will further prey on the Target. Show up at the Target's social events, workplaces, and homes, insisting they need the Target, or making some other excuse. If that does not suffice, the Pulpit Predator will resort to other tactics like manipulation, fear, and even force. Manipulation is not always direct, but the Pulpit Predator will use it when they have been materially generous or helped the Target in any way. This is part of the grooming process to get the Target feeling obligated and go beyond their normal inhibitions.

The event will undoubtedly create scars. The Target is forever changed to some degree. While some Targets recover from events, there are those who can't seem to find their way back and resort to other self-destructed behavior. A Target should never be told to just get over the event. Scars from the events have no expiration date, and even when processed, in therapy, godly counsel, with friends and family, or internally, triggers can produce emotional responses in the Target again and again well after the event has stopped. Since events are about gaining control, the Pulpit Predator orchestrates the events to have the greatest impact in the shortest amount of time with the longest effect. Every Target needs prayer, assistance, and love. Reach out to someone to talk to. My contact information will be included at the back of the book if you want to reach out and talk. I see you, I hear you, I love you, and I pray this helps you heal.

~ 6 ~

THE CYCLE

There is a cycle with Clergy Sexual Misconduct or CSM. Since it is cyclical, it can be duplicated and reoccurring, thus making it so hard to believe when it concerns adults and adolescents. Adult Targets are mislabeled as mistresses and thought to be engaged in affairs. However, **coercion is not consent**. That would be like saying a rape survivor is guilty of seducing a rapist, although survivors have been accused of such.

If an individual pursues a leader, the leader is in a position of power and has the moral responsibility and authority to handle the situation accordingly. The matter should be brought to the attention of the oversight committee. The pursuer should be confronted in the presence of witnesses and, if need be, in front of the entire congregation. Leaders are not given a license to engage in Clergy Sexual Misconduct. On the contrary, they have been licensed to uphold Biblical righteousness. A license that is sometimes misused for selfish gain.

Clergy Sexual Misconduct happens in correlation with spiritual abuse. Spiritual abuse, as defined in an article by Lee Gatiss, is "A systematic pattern of behavior which causes serious alarm and daily distress, perhaps with a threat of violence of some sort, in a church context or within a religious relationship or organization." It is this systematic pattern of behavior that creates the cycle. Cycles of abuse create trauma, and trauma amplifies the cycle of abuse. Unless there is outside intervention, the cycle continues.

The cycle involves the Pulpit Predator identifying a Target's weakness, exploiting that weakness, getting the Target to engage in sin, maintaining control using guilt and shame, and lastly, destruction. The cycle can and often is repetitive, creating an unnatural bond. Erica Laub, LICSW, lists the seven stages of trauma bonding as Love Bombing, Trust & Dependency, Criticism, Manipulation & Gaslighting, Resignation & Giving Up, Loss of Self, and Addiction to the Cycle.

Let's define them as the following:

1. Love Bombing - Using high praise and excessive flattery to create a "we" relationship, often made to look like the Pulpit Predator is oblivious to wrong-doing. This stage causes the Target to let down their

guard and trust the intentions of a Pulpit Predator.

2. Trust and Dependency - Building on the illusion of trust, the Target is often tested of their trust and dependency on the Pulpit Predator and made to feel guilty if they have doubts. At this point, the Pulpit Predator has met the Target's material, financial, or emotional needs.

3. Criticism - The Target's qualities or character are labeled as insignificant or problematic through criticism. What once was praised as an asset now has the Target questioning themselves, apologizing for their gifts and talents, and changing their beliefs and behavior.

4. Manipulation and Gaslighting - Both are psychological abuse used to get the Target to question their reality or perception of what is happening. The Pulpit Predator is never fully honest or takes full responsibility for their behavior but instead shifts that blame to the Target. Comments like, "After all I have done to help you, I feel betrayed that you don't trust me." "My spouse doesn't understand me like you do, which is why I can only talk to you about _____." Or, "I wouldn't feel like this if you weren't_____." Fill in the blanks. These are only a few examples, but they all shift blame.

5. Resignation and Giving Up - As typical with all

cycles of abuse, the Target eventually gives in. Not in the form of consent but engaging in people-pleasing behavior and avoiding conflict, especially if some form of threats have been made. Because of the extent of psychological and spiritual abuse, red flags are ignored or missed altogether. The Target will usually blame themselves for the Pulpit Predator's inappropriate behavior.

6. Loss of Self - Loss of identity and personal boundaries leaves the Target disconnected from their previous life. The loss is progressive, and the Pulpit Predator will go to great lengths to keep the Target isolated or in a controlled environment. The Pulpit Predator often uses a Partner to knowingly or unknowingly keep tabs on the Target, reporting to the Pulpit Predator. Isolated in shame, loss of confidence and self-esteem, and struggling with guilt, the Target could rely on the Partner as a confidant. Over time, it becomes more and more difficult for the Target to escape the cycle or even want to.

7. Addiction to the Cycle - In this stage, the Pulpit Predator returns to stage one of love bombing and further deepens the trauma experienced by the Target. The cycle continues and is normalized. By this stage, the Target takes all responsibility. Guilt, shame, and blame are reinforced as the process continues. The unnatural bond keeps the Target desiring step 1, and they see no escape.

This trauma takes a psychological toll and can also manifest in physical forms. Post-Traumatic Stress Disorder is common with Targets who often can't leave the cycle without outside influence. Once the cycle is broken, healing can begin, but the Target is vulnerable to returning feeling unwanted outside of the cycle.

Within the church culture, it can be challenging for the Target to break the cycle because of fear of damage to the church. The Pulpit Predator will use that fear to control the Target with statements like, "The future of the church depends on you" or "You have the power to destroy this church." Comments like these suggest the Target has power over the Pulpit Predator and cycle, further deepening the guilt and shame. The troubling thing is those statements are factual, at least in part. If the Target exposes the cycle of abuse, they are often labeled and even blamed by other church members. If the Pulpit Predator is the pastor, the Target is accused of ruining the pastor's life and career. It can take years before a Pulpit Predator is removed. It usually takes multiple Targets before the issue is addressed. Churches have shut down, congregations split, and some have walked away from their faith because a Target was brave enough to expose CSM, the cycle of abuse, and Pulpit Predator.

The abuse is covered up if the cycle is embedded within the church culture. Even if there are multiple Targets, it can be difficult to change the culture of that environment. The culture rarely changes if there is no righteous oversight committee or governing board, and the Pulpit Predator can move on to the next Target. Due to the lack of protection, most Targets prefer to forget about the experience; therefore, they often never share about the abuse. Because of unnatural bonding, Targets may stay in that church. No one heals in that toxic environment. You could look around your congregation, and a Target may be seated next to you. See the cycle and call it what it is. ABUSE!

Adonai is near those with broken hearts; he saves those whose spirit is crushed. Psalms 34:19 CJB

~ 7 ~

THE WOUNDED

The events of spiritual and sexual abuse hurt more than just the Target. The Church, the body of believers in Jesus, are the Wounded, indirectly affected by the events. Some in the church assume the role of Partners but are mainly just as blindsided as the Target. Yes, blindsided; as Traci Scott puts it, "Congregations are considered safe sanctuaries, so congregants are more likely to let down their guard with religious leaders than they would with others." Safe places are supposed to be just that, safe. When a place of worship is robbed of that by the Pulpit Predator, all types of evil can inflict deep wounds, often called church hurt.

Church hurt can shake the core of one's faith and trust in the church and sometimes even in God himself. When Pulpit Predators are exposed, the Wounded often blame themselves for not recognizing the Pulpit Predator and for not speaking up or leaving when they witnessed

Biblical errors. Like the Target, the Wounded can be shuffled through an entirely different process. It may start the same but not end as extreme as that of the Target. The process of desensitizing makes Biblically incorrect and uncomfortable things comfortable and sometimes tolerable. Pulpit Predators manipulate the Word of God for their selfish gain. When a Pulpit Predator seeks financial gain, the entire congregation becomes the Target. Before condemning all aspects of giving and finances in the church, particularly for church staff, let's get an understanding. Pastors and church leaders are entitled to a salary, accept honorariums, write and sell books, and even host events.

Elders who do their work well should be respected and paid well, especially those who work hard at both preaching and teaching. For the Scripture says, "You must not muzzle an ox to keep it from eating as it treads out the grain." And in another place, "Those who work deserve their pay!" 1 Timothy 5:17-18 NLT

Not financially providing for the church staff would be disrespectful and unbiblical. It would be as if you and I went to work and never received pay because the boss decided that our gifts and talents that benefited their company were from God and should be given for free. We are all called to work either in the church or the marketplace; the location of where we work should not determine whether or not we are paid. With that being said, the problem occurs when the Scripture mentioned above, and others like it, are misused by the Pulpit Predator, who ventures over to coercion for their personal gain. The Wounded are led to believe they are honoring the pastor when actually they are being manipulated.

The Wounded are not ignorant or uneducated; they come from all walks of life and various economic and social backgrounds. When under the proper pastoral care, they thrive, but when the Pulpit Predator is the caretaker, the Wounded are negatively impacted in all areas of life. There is often a shift from worship directed toward God to that of the Pulpit Predator. Placing them on pedestals they were never intended to be on, but because the Pulpit Predator relishes in arrogance, redirecting the Wounded back to God never occurs. If the Pulpit Predator is well known, it amplifies the situation.

Spiritual abuse is using any Biblical principle and spiritual authority out of context to guide a person or group of persons to an outcome outside of their own will. From the "volunteer" who is told they cannot miss a service without informing the pastor with a valid excuse and to the proverbial "God told me to tell you____," fill in the blank, all with the intent to keep a person doing the will of the Pulpit Predator. And yes, I experienced both. As I write this, I think, "How gullible was I?" I could fill another book with things I was told, experienced, or did in the name of pleasing God when I was actually pleasing man. This sense of needing to be accepted was a misdirected wound already in me. My mentor says that when you seek a rescuer, you will always find an oppressor, and my life has proven that to be true. People pleasing in the name of serving God is a religious mindset that is anti-God and rooted in fear, and the Pulpit Predator knows it. The pastor, male or female, is to be respected, NOT worshipped.

When the Wounded finally realizes what has happened, discord and divisions occur. You are then left with a few groups of people: those who choose to back the Pulpit Predator, those who choose to expose and hold them accountable, and those so wounded they leave the church altogether. Discord and division lead to church hurt. Church hurt leads to broken relationships between congregants, friends, and families inflicted in the church and trust issues caused by those in church leadership. Church hurt are profound wounds and challenging to heal. Why? Because the hurting comes to the church seeking to be healed from painful life situations or poor decision-making. They seek hope and a sense of peace, family, and fellowship, and when they encounter further hurt, it inflicts additional wounds and scars that become sealed in what I like to call spiritual cement.

Where do you go when the church hurts you? That is what makes it all so devastating. The place or thing you turn to after church hurt is not always the safest place. There is a mental and spiritual battle that must be conquered. Acknowledging is the beginning of the process; without it, the Wounded stay wounded no matter where they go.

PAUSE! Before you move to the next chapter, think of all the times you have been hurt in the church. A snide comment here, a blatant lie there, and manipulation to the third degree. That which started as a slight prick festered into a full-fledged gaping wound oozing the puss of unforgiveness. Deal with it right here, right now. You may not extend forgiveness now, but you can lay the offense at the feet of the Messiah. That wound will not heal itself; it is too big for you to do alone. Together, let's heal.

~ 8 ~

THE BYSTANDER

Bystanders, well, they are the ones outside of the church environment. They are those who are nonbelievers or those who have decided that church was not for them. Although not part of the church, they are watching the behaviors and mannerisms of the church. After all, the church is the representative of God. When I say church, I am not referring to the building; however, the building is important. It is the building in which the Bystander enters or is invited and is introduced to Jesus. Those seeking God and entering the building for the first time are vulnerable to what they are about to experience. Those early visits and interactions form an opinion and later decision to follow God. Whatever they have experienced in their lives up to that point is vital information about their spiritual need. In the hands of a healthy church and pastor, that information can help develop the Bystander in their relationship with God, find spiritual resources and counsel, and create community. In the hands of the Pulpit Predator, this information is ammunition.

The Pulpit Predator has gained knowledge to seek out the next Target. Some pastors have created a predatory culture in the church to which the Bystander is subjected. Most Bystanders can pick up on the culture within a particular congregation; they feel the vibe. They have just entered in and are therefore not bewildered by the Pulpit Predator, having a more objective view; however, if a Bystander stays for an extended period in that culture, they will normalize it. I saw it in the beginning, at least in part. There was something in the culture that seemed off, but because I was dealing with so many personal issues, pain, and the fact that I was new, I just settled in. I had family there, so surely it was a safe place to be, or so I thought. After a time, I just began normalizing things that should have been red flags.

Bystanders don't always separate the people in the church from God. If the culture is corrupt, the Bystander can assume that all churches have the same culture. Instead of seeing the Pulpit Predator as the issue, God becomes the issue. This mindset changes the world's view of the Church and the God it says it serves.

As the collective Church, we have been called to make disciples. We are to introduce the Bystanders to Jesus for salvation and then disciple them in their walk with Him.

The Pulpit Predator and the corrupt church culture make it challenging to fulfill the commission Jesus gave:

Then Jesus came close to them and said, "All the authority of the universe has been given to me. Now go in my authority and make disciples of all nations, baptizing them in the name of the Father, the Son, and the Holy Spirit. And teach them to faithfully follow all that I have commanded you. And never forget that I am with you every day, even to the completion of this age." **Matthew 28:18-20 TPT**

It is difficult to teach the command and principles of God that we want the Bystander to uphold when the Pulpit Predator is not living up to those standards and has created a toxic and dismissive environment of those same principles.

Now, let me say that healthy churches are not perfect, but healthy churches have healthy cultural environments. Bystanders, Wounded, and Targets can grow, heal, and recover in these environments. Every church should constantly check the temperature and health of their environment. To think you have a healthy church without such checks is arrogance and the breeding ground for the Dragon.

One issue with checking the health of church culture is when churches ask their leaders and congregants for a health evaluation. That is all good to a certain extent because if a church is toxic, it was the leaders who allowed it to remain that way. Asking them is like asking the Dragon if he is playing fair. Seeking the actual temperature of the culture should come from outside of the environment. No matter how many times I place my hand on my forehead to see if I have a fever, I can only get an accurate answer if I use an outside instrument, a thermometer. The instrument for healthy church examination is the Bible.

Jesus gave a parable to his disciples: the parable of the sower. The sower, however, is not the emphasis of the story. The focus is on the seed but, ultimately, the soil, which determines the health of what grew from it. The seed is the individual, such as the Bystander, and the soil represents the church culture. Let's have a look.

That same day Jesus went out of the house and sat by the lake. Such large crowds gathered around him that he got into a boat and sat in it, while all the people stood on the shore. Then he told them many things in parables, saying: "A farmer went out to sow his seed. As he was scattering the seed, some fell along the path, and the birds came and ate it up. Some fell on rocky places, where it did not have much soil. It sprang up quickly, because the soil was shallow. But when the sun came up, the plants were scorched, and they withered because they had no root. Other seed fell among thorns, which grew up and choked the plants. Still other seed fell on good soil, where it produced a crop—a hundred, sixty or thirty times what was sown. **Matthew 13:1-8 NIV**

"Listen then to what the parable of the sower means: When anyone hears the message about the kingdom and does not understand it, the evil one comes and snatches away what was sown in their heart. This is the seed sown along the path. The seed falling on rocky ground refers to someone who hears the word and at once receives it with joy. But since they have no root, they last only a short time. When trouble or persecution comes because of the word, they quickly fall away. The seed falling among the thorns refers to someone who hears the word, but the worries of this life and the deceitfulness of wealth choke the word, making it unfruitful. But the seed falling on good soil refers to someone who hears the word and understands it. This is the one who produces a crop, yielding a hundred, sixty or thirty times what was sown." **Matthew 13:18-23 NIV**

In our modern day, the church is the primary place to hear the message about the Kingdom. The church must be healthy. So let me say this to every Bystander. I'm sorry we have not always been the best representative of God. He is far greater than we could ever represent, but we have the task of getting better at it. This is my commitment to you to do a better job of helping to create healthy church cultures.

Be well balanced and always alert, because your enemy, the devil, roams around incessantly, like a roaring lion looking for its prey to devour. Take a decisive stand against him and resist his every attack with strong, vigorous faith. For you know that your believing brothers and sisters around the world are experiencing the same kinds of troubles you endure. 1 Peter 5:8-9 TPT

~ 9 ~

THE DRAGON

The Dragon is the Adversary (Satan), and the Wounded has always been his actual Target. He has no desire for the Wounded to grow, thrive, and most certainly not be healthy. His mission is to see that the Wounded are broken and dysfunctional, constantly in discord and not walking in their purpose. The Bystander he desires to hold onto, keeping their hearts from finding peace in a relationship with our Heavenly Father. His attempt to destroy an individual Target is a strategic move to isolate a threat and silence its voice. The Pulpit Predator and Partner are pawns in his hands.

The game the Dragon plays is calculated, and he leaves nothing to chance. While he is not all-knowing or all-powerful, he does rely on others for information and demons to yield to his doings. His arsenal has no new tricks, but he is crafty enough to disguise them. "Did God really say..." (Genesis 3:1) You find this question behind every deception. He is always challenging the authority of the Healer. His beef is not with the Wounded, Target, Bystander, Partner, or Pulpit Predator. It's with God. The Dragon has this wild imagination that he can be equal to God. That imagination got him banned from his home and who he was created to be: a divine being, an angel, beautiful in every way, so stop envisioning a pitchfork and horns. He doesn't want his original position back; he wants the entire Kingdom—the Kingdom of Heaven.

The Dragon knows full well that he is no match for the Healer. His game plan is to get back at Him by hurting what the Healer loves the most, humankind, created in His image, His children. What father wouldn't be in pain when his children are hurt? Hurt the children, and you hurt the Father. So, how does he hurt the children? Divide and conquer or, in other words, steal, kill, and destroy. (John 10:10)

Watch the strategy:

- Keep as many as he can from knowing the Healer. How? Silence all Targets and all those that proclaim the Truth.

But how can they call on someone if they haven't trusted in him? And how can they trust in someone if they haven't heard about him? And how can they hear about someone if no one is proclaiming him? And how can people proclaim him unless God sends them?—as the Tanakh puts it, "How beautiful are the feet of those announcing good news about good things!" **Romans 10:14-15 CJB**

- Keep the Wounded weak. How? Sow discord, chaos, confusion, and especially division. Nonessential arguments between denominations. Diluted doctrine and false teachers.

Jesus knew their thoughts and said to them, "Every kingdom divided against itself will be ruined, and every city or household divided against itself will not stand. **Matthew 12:25 CJB**

- Keep the Bystander entangled in spirituality but never the Healer. Following the systems of this world.

For although they knew God, they neither glorified him as God nor gave thanks to him, but their thinking became futile and their foolish hearts were darkened. Although they claimed to be wise, they became fools and exchanged the glory of the immortal God for images made to look like a mortal human being and birds and animals and reptiles. Therefore God gave them over in the sinful desires of their hearts to sexual impurity for the degrading of their bodies with one another. They exchanged the truth about God for a lie, and worshiped and served created things rather than the Creator—who is forever praised. Amen. **Romans 1:21-25 NIV**

- Keep the Pulpit Predator and Partner in pursuit of selfish ambition, recognition, and full of pride. A Partner with an orphan spirit that seeks the approval of man.

Who among you is wise and understanding? Let him demonstrate it by his good way of life, by actions done in the humility that grows out of wisdom. But if you harbor in your hearts bitter jealousy and selfish ambition, don't boast and attack the truth with lies! This wisdom is not the kind that comes down from above; on the contrary, it is worldly, unspiritual, demonic. For where there are jealousy and selfish ambition, there will be disharmony and every foul practice. **James 3:13-16 CJB**

Peter and the other apostles replied: "We must obey God rather than human beings! **Acts 5:29 NIV**

The Dragon only knows one thing, and that is the Kingdom of Heaven, so he mimics it. He has established the kingdom of darkness on the earth and has been given authority to reign for a short time. His kingdom is limited and ends in death; he knows it. And since we know it is the Dragon behind all the pain in "church hurt," we understand that it is spiritual warfare. The Pulpit Predator became a pawn in the hands of the Dragon to wreak havoc within the community of God and the ministries God has set forth. Although the Dragon has caused a disruption in the congregations, his power can not disrupt the Kingdom of Heaven. He can't stop the Healer from restoring and healing. Although we know this to be true, the Dragon is relentless in his attempts. We must be vigilant in our spiritual battle, understanding that our war isn't against flesh and blood, and neither is this book.

Now my beloved ones, I have saved these most important truths for last: Be supernaturally infused with strength through your life union with the Lord Jesus. Stand victorious with the force of his explosive power flowing in and through you. Put on God's complete set of armor provided for us, so that you will be protected as you fight against the evil strategies of the accuser! Your hand-to-hand combat is not with human beings, but with the highest principalities and authorities operating in rebellion under the heavenly realms. For they are a powerful class of demon-gods and evil spirits that hold this dark world in bondage. Because of this, you must wear all the armor that God provides so you're protected as you confront the slanderer, for you are destined for all things and will rise victorious. Put on truth as a belt to strengthen you to stand in triumph. Put on holiness as the protective armor that covers your heart. Stand on your feet alert, then you'll always be ready to share the blessings of peace. In every battle, take faith as your wrap-around shield, for it is able to extinguish the blazing arrows coming at you from the Evil One! Embrace the power of salvation's full deliverance, like a helmet to protect your thoughts from lies. And take the mighty razor-sharp Spirit-sword of the spoken Word of God. Pray passionately in the Spirit, as you constantly intercede with every form of prayer at all times. Pray the blessings of God upon all his believers. Ephesians 6:10-18 TPT

And in another translation.

Finally, be strong in the Lord and in his mighty power. Put on the full armor of God, so that you can take your stand against the devil's schemes. For our struggle is not against flesh and blood, but against the rulers, against the authorities, against the powers of this dark world and against the spiritual forces of evil in the heavenly realms. Therefore put on the full armor of God, so that when the day of evil comes, you may be able to stand your ground, and after you have done everything, to stand. Stand firm then, with the belt of truth buckled around your waist, with the breastplate of righteousness in place, and with your feet fitted with the readiness that comes from the gospel of peace. In addition to all this, take up the shield of faith, with which you can extinguish all the flaming arrows of the evil one. Take the helmet of salvation and the sword of the Spirit, which is the word of God. And pray in the Spirit on all occasions with all kinds of prayers and requests. With this in mind, be alert and always keep on praying for all the Lord's people. Ephesians 6:10-18 NIV

Now that we know the true predator in the pulpit, we can band together and fight. Just because we know that the Dragon will ultimately lose this battle doesn't mean we sit back and do nothing as a community of believers. Take up your weapon and fight. Be as relentless as God's enemy. Fight for the Target to regain their voice. Fight for the Wounded to be healthy. Fight for the Bystander to encounter the one true God. Fight for the Partner to have opened eyes. Fight even for the Pulpit Predator, who has been deceived into thinking they are above reproach, to repent and return to their first love. The Healer!

~ 10 ~

THE HEALER

Before you can get to the hurt, you must chisel away all the spiritual cement. There is only one who can chisel and not cause additional harm. Yahweh, The Host High, our Heavenly Father! Yes, God uses others in our lives to bring about healing, like therapists and doctors, but the orchestrator of healing is God himself. There isn't one person impacted by Pulpit Predators that does not need healing. The Targets, the Wounded, the Bystander, the Partners, and even the Pulpit Predator all need the deepest healing that comes from not only a relationship with God but intimacy with God.

Intimacy with God goes beyond church pew knowledge. It's a desire to grow, understand, and seek God, surrendering to His plan for our lives. The refreshing flow from the healing, loving arms of a good Father begins to heal the heart. We have been given an invitation to come close to God.

"Are you tired? Worn out? Burned out on religion? Come to me. Get away with me and you'll recover your life. I'll show you how to take a real rest. Walk with me and work with me—watch how I do it. Learn the unforced rhythms of grace. I won't lay anything heavy or ill-fitting on you. Keep company with me and you'll learn to live freely and lightly." **Matthew 11:28-30 The Message**

The invitation is just that, an invitation. We can either remain in the place of the hurt or accept the invitation to be healed. Accepting God's healing requires action. In the verse above, Jesus gives the instructions to "come." Coming means we must acknowledge a few things that may be shameful and painful—memories that we may have buried or things that we have done amid all the madness. Even then, God still pleads for us to come to Him. We can't escape the love of the Healer; we can't outrun it. Nothing we have done or that was done to us cancels that love. I love how Paul, the apostle, explains it.

For I am convinced that neither death nor life, nor angels nor principalities, nor things present nor things to come, nor powers, nor height nor depth, nor any other created thing will be able to separate us from the love of God that is in Messiah Yeshua our Lord. **Romans 8:38-39 TLV**

Jehovah Rophe. That is the name that Moses introduced us to in Exodus 15—the Lord who Heals. Every name of God exemplifies a character of God. What I love about

God is that He can never deny who He is. When He reveals a name, He reveals an aspect of Himself that will never change and benefits those who call upon Him. Healing is the very nature of God. Unfortunately, we have done the names of God a disservice by reducing them to just names. We like to say them but fail to understand their power entirely.

To understand the intent of God revealing the name Jehovah Rophe, we need to look at the context in which God first revealed it. The children of Israel had been delivered from the hands of Egyptian bondage. After singing an elaborate song of praise to God for delivering them, they wandered around for three days in the wilderness. They were thirsty, understandably so, and human nature kicked in. The song began to fade, giving way to complaining and blaming. God had performed so many miracles to get them to this place, but all they could focus on was the current needs of their flesh. Their complaining began at a place called Marah.

Marah was an oasis. Amid all the dryness, dust, and barrenness, they stumbled upon a fertile, green place with abundant water as a refuge for their needs. Here's the thing about Marah, it held up to its name, bitter. The water was undrinkable because of the bitterness, and the people turned on Moses. It was in this place of bitterness God revealed an aspect of Himself that there had yet to be a need for. Isn't that just like God, to show Himself when we need Him most, exactly how we need to see Him. He could have given this name long ago when they were in famine, bondage, and fear, but no, He waited. He waited until their mouths revealed what was hidden in their hearts, bitterness. What was His cure for the bitterness in Marah's oasis and of man's heart? A piece of wood, but not just any wood. A specific piece of wood.

A piece of wood in a place of bitterness was God's answer to both a physical and spiritual need. Moses chucked the wood into the water, which became drinkable, giving it a life-sustaining resource. But, it was about more than drinking water; it was a picture of what would come. God would use a piece of wood to deal with the bitter heart of humanity once and for all. The cross! When God said I am Jehovah Rophe, it was about the heart, not the water. There was a healing that needed to take place before they moved on. Rophe meant more than just healing; it was restoration, repair, mending, wholeness, and a cure. Think of a doctor with all the training and skills needed. They spend countless hours learning how to diagnose, mend or repair, giving medicine to heal, and seeking cures. Doctors can have all sorts of specialties to cover all aspects of human life, physical, mental, emotional, and even spiritual. In all their specialties, they are limited and expensive. Jehovah Rophe is all that and so much more.

The children of Israel now had a Great Physician, and they would need to use that name many times, just as we do. Once that lesson was done and His name was revealed, they moved on. They landed in another oasis, Elim, only this time they found 12 streams, all drinkable. Elim, too held up to its name, meaning strong tree with its seventy palm trees and full vegetation. The children of Israel had experienced Jehovah Rophe firsthand, which played a massive role in their lives from that moment on. Several more times in the Old Testament was that name used to call upon God.

Today, no matter if you are the Target, Partner, Wounded, Bystander, or Pulpit Predator, Jehovah Rophe is here to heal you. He alone is the only one that can heal the deepest wounds of church hurt. He will not force healing upon us, but we will find it if we seek it. The Healer does not want us to remain in the pain of events. We learn valuable lessons that we will forever remember, but the pain must go. Pain will never disappear on its own. It must be confronted and then released. Jehovah Rophe knows how to help us face that pain so that we do not create more pain for ourselves or anyone else. Confrontation does not necessarily mean we must sit down with the Pulpit Predator or Partner and force them to apologize. It means that we must confront our emotions about the event, being completely honest with ourselves and God. We must deal with any anger and bitterness in our hearts towards the Pulpit Predator, Partner, ourselves, and God.

We will never seek Jehovah Rophe if we are angry with Him. That is the hope of the Dragon. The most amazing thing is Jehovah Rophe will seek us even when we are angry with Him. When the children of Israel were angry in Marah, God came to meet them. He can handle whatever resentment we may have towards Him. While He didn't cause the event that wounded you, He didn't stop it either. That is a tough pill to swallow at times. It's that difficulty that creates questions we wrestle with in our minds: God, where were you? Why did this happen to me? If God is all-powerful, why didn't He stop this? Does God really love me? We can get lost in the circle of questions that we may not get an answer to on this side of heaven. What I do know is that God is love, another name, and another characteristic, and He can not stop being who He is. He IS love. I sense Jehovah Rophe saying, I know you are hurting and in pain. I know you have questions that you can't find the answers to, and I know that you are angry even with Me, but I love you. I AM here to heal you.

Before you move on to the next section of this book, stop and sit with this for a moment. Sit with Jehovah Rophe for as long as it takes to connect with your Healer. Sit until you sense the weight of His presence and love. Sit until you acknowledge the pain and allow your heart to be set free from the guilt and shame. Forgiving is a process for us humans; you may not be ready to visit that, and it's okay. Sit with every emotion that comes up, and when it does, name it and connect it to an event, then place it in the hands of the Healer. (Example: I am sad/ that the lies have divided our congregation/I place this in Your hands Jehovah Rophe) I'll be honest with you; this will take time and can be emotionally draining, but it will free you. Speak it out or write it out, but whatever you do, don't hold it in any longer. Whether you realize it or not, it is destroying you and everything around you. God wants you healed up, not held back.

I AM Jehovah Rophe, the Lord who heals you.

God uses different methods to heal. Just as a doctor will use various treatments depending on what is ailing you, The Healer chooses the best method for you. For some, it is speaking to a trusted friend; for others, it is meditating on Scripture. There are times when healing comes through processing the issue in therapy. I have heard many excuses for why believers should not seek therapy, and none made any sense. Seeking therapy is not a lack of faith in God's ability. Professional counseling, therapy, inpatient or outpatient, whatever the case may be, is a tool God may use in the healing process. The stigma of mental health has prevented many people of faith from receiving the help they need. Help that could prevent the cycle of pain and abuse.

If you had a child who broke their leg and was in great pain, would you tuck them into bed out of fear that someone may think you lacked faith? Of course not; you would get the help your child needed. When dealing with issues of the heart and mind, there is a brokenness that needs to be mended. Depression and anxiety are real, and those in the faith community are not exempt from dealing with them. The Pulpit Predator, Partner, Target, Wounded, and even the Bystander may all need, at some point, professional help to process and overcome what has happened to them or what they have done to hurt others. Know this: The Healer chooses how to heal.

I want to give you some Scripture references on healing. These may be helpful and bring comfort, but one thing they will definitely do is ground you in truth. The biggest lie of the Dragon is to get you to think that The Healer has abandoned you. That you are in too much pain or that you have caused too much harm for The Healer to do anything for you. Even when we know that is not the case, convincing ourselves not to listen can be challenging. The longer we listen to the Dragon, the easier it becomes to believe the lie. The opposite is just as true. The longer you listen, meditate, and speak the Word of Truth, the easier it becomes to reject the lie. The Healer wants you healed. Totally healed? Yes, but we have to be willing to roll up our sleeves and put in some work.

Is anyone among you suffering? Let him pray. Is anyone cheerful? Let him sing praises. Is anyone among you sick? Let him call for the elders of Messiah's community, and let them pray over him, anointing him with oil in the name of the Lord. The prayer of faith will save the one who is sick, and the Lord will raise him up. If he has committed sins, he will be forgiven. So confess your offenses to one another and pray for one another so that you may be healed. The effective prayer of a righteous person is very powerful...My brothers and sisters, if any among you strays from the truth and someone turns him back, let him know that the one who turns a sinner from the error of his way shall save a soul from death and cover a multitude of sins. James 5:13-16; 19-20 TLV

He heals the brokenhearted and bandages their wounds. Psalms 147:3 NLT

So they cried out to Adonai in their distress, and He delivered them out of their troubles. He sent His word and healed them, and rescued them from their pits. Psalms 107:19-20 TLV

Suddenly, a man with leprosy approached him and knelt before him. "Lord," the man said, "if you are willing, you can heal me and make me clean." Jesus reached out and touched him. "I am willing," he said. "Be healed!" And instantly the leprosy disappeared. Matthew 8:2-3 NLT

BLESS (AFFECTIONATELY, gratefully praise) the Lord, O my soul; and all that is [deepest] within me, bless His holy name! Bless (affectionately, gratefully praise) the Lord, O my soul, and forget not [one of] all His benefits— Who forgives [every one of] all your iniquities, Who heals [each one of] all your diseases, Who redeems your life from the pit and corruption, Who beautifies, dignifies, and crowns you with loving-kindness and tender mercy; Who satisfies your mouth [your necessity and desire at your personal age and situation] with good so that your youth, renewed, is like the eagle's [strong, overcoming, soaring]! Psalms 103:1-5 AMP

My child, pay attention to what I say. Listen carefully to my words. Don't lose sight of them. Let them penetrate deep into your heart, for they bring life to those who find them, and healing to their whole body. Guard your heart above all else, for it determines the course of your life. Proverbs 4:20-23 NLT

He said, "If you will listen carefully to the voice of the Lord your God and do what is right in his sight, obeying his commands and keeping all his decrees, then I will not make you suffer any of the diseases I sent on the Egyptians; for I am the Lord who heals you." Exodus 15:26 NLT

The Healer is often viewed as a vengeful deity far off in the distance, raining down judgment on all those who sneeze wrong. We tend to be like Adam and Eve and run away from the one we should be running to. Why is that? Shame and guilt. Oh, how those two words bring a lifetime of regrets and missed opportunities. Let me share some truth with you. Yahweh is a Father, unlike any father we have ever met. And depending on your relationship with your earthly father, your view of God may not reflect the best image of His character.

We understand that He is a good Father, but we don't fully understand that He is **our** good Father. There is a vast difference between "a" Father and "our" Father. Father becomes personal when we declare Him as ours. This is what makes the verses in Matthew 6 so amazing. When the disciples asked Jesus to teach them to pray, He personalized prayer, which was something that was not done. Imagine the God of the universe being intimate with you and me. It was borderline scandalous.

But you, when you pray, go into your room, close the door, and pray to your Father in secret. Your Father, who sees what is done in secret, will reward you. "And when you pray, don't babble on and on like the pagans, who think God will hear them better if they talk a lot. Don't be like them, because your Father knows what you need before you ask him. You, therefore, pray like this: 'Our Father in heaven! May your Name be kept holy. May your Kingdom come, your will be done on earth as in heaven. Give us the food we need today. Forgive us what we have done wrong, as we, too, have forgiven those who have wronged us. And do not lead us into hard testing, but keep us safe from the Evil One. For kingship, power and glory are yours forever. Amen.' Matthew 6:6-13 CJB

Out the gate, Yeshua teaches us that the Father is ours. Enter into your Father's healing. He is our Abba. Enter into His embrace for you. One of my favorite Scriptures is found in John chapter 17.

And eternal life is this: to know you, the one true God, and him whom you sent, Yeshua the Messiah. John 17:3 CJB

When Jesus prays those words, he uses language often used when a man is intimate with his wife. Real life, eternal life, is a perfectly complete union with the Father. He so desperately wanted you that He gave up His son.

Run to the Father. Fall into the arms of your Healer and be healed.

~ 11 ~

THE PIECES

The aftermath of Clergy Sexual Misconduct is shards everywhere; broken pieces must be put back together again. Everyone heals at a different pace. Healing is a journey, not a marathon, and it is personal. Just like healing, forgiveness is a process. The Target and Wounded will fluctuate in their emotions. Feel how you feel because feelings are based on your experience; therefore, no one can tell you they are false. When you are ready, enter the phase of forgiveness.

Forgiving yourself, whether you are the Target, the Wounded, or the Bystander, will be the easiest to do. You are not sitting in the seat of the accused. You are a witness and Target of victimization. Your broken pieces are the smallest of all shards. Finding all the pieces that need to be mended will take time. Once you do, mourning will take place. Mourning the loss of who you were before this all happened. You may be better after healing, but you will never be the same. Mended pieces still have cracks.

Forgiving God may be a little harder to do, depending on the level you hold Him responsible. You may have been taught that being angry with God is not Christian-like. I tell you, it is human-like. I don't believe that the God who gave us an array of emotions would tell us to stuff them when it comes to Him. After all, He knows how we feel anyway. Anger is a God-given emotion. I'm an advocate of being extremely honest with God. And yes, I have yelled at Him several times during this process. Don't let anyone condemn you for doing so. I don't fully understand, but He gave us free will, and with that, we jack things up, but pain has never been His desire for us. This doesn't lessen God's love for you, and it shouldn't lessen your love for God.

Forgiving the Dragon is never to be considered. I don't need to write much more than that. He stands accused, is guilty of all charges, and will suffer punishment.

Forgiving the Partner is hard. It could be as hard as forgiving the Pulpit Predator if the Partner played an active role. If they were ignorant, I pray this opens their eyes. Trust has been destroyed and must be earned. Restoring that relationship is a personal choice you are not required to make. I have yet to make that choice. Here, forgiveness is making a choice not to be resentful.

Forgiving the Pulpit Predator is the hardest of them

all. I know you want to be pissed off forever. I did. T.D. Jakes says, "I think the first step is to understand that forgiveness does not exonerate the perpetrator. Forgiveness liberates the victim. It's a gift you give yourself." I partially agree; remember, I was a Target, not a victim. Forgiveness does not negate accountability. Let me say it a little louder. **PULPIT PREDATORS SHOULD BE HELD ACCOUNTABLE**. See, yelling is still ok, even after you have forgiven. When it comes to the Pulpit Predator, I have the right to be angry and resentful, and so do you, but I choose not to be. We have a right to seek justice. I realized that forgiving the Pulpit Predator was not about excusing his behavior, releasing him from accountability, or sweeping it under the rug. It is not about letting him back into my life. Never! Choosing to forgive meant I acknowledged that he owed me a debt he could never repay. His apology, public announcement to the congregation, beg for forgiveness, or monetary settlement, none of which I have received, could cover what he owed. I was robbed of my time, self-esteem, my voice, and so much more, which he could never give back. I choose to forgive because I refuse to give him one more ounce of my time, emotions, or thoughts of doing him bodily harm. Yep, I went there. This book is my time to you, not him or the Dragon. I will never forget, but I am not responsible for his actions, nor am I responsible for his judgment. He doesn't get to dictate my freedom or my journey beyond trauma. I am responsible for my victory.

AND THIS IS MY VICTORY!

THE END!

Wait! Did you really think I would just leave you right there? Of course not. This is about healing, and healing is practical. So, let's take action and **repair** what's broken.

~ 12 ~

THE REPAIR

This chapter is challenging for me to write. While some of the others were difficult emotionally, this chapter requires that I walk a fine line with a word no one may be ready to hear. Although I have mentioned the word before, it is necessary that I lay it open before you. That word is FORGIVENESS. I might have just made you cringe if you are the Target or the Wounded. I understand that word is a trigger to some who have experienced trauma. This is not the place where I tell you that you must forgive. It is, however, the place where I share the repair that brings healing. How we can roll up our sleeves and work towards forgiveness. Forgiveness is a personal road in the repair process. That road is one that the Healer delights to walk you down, but not even He will force you down it. So please don't allow anyone else to force you down it, not even me.

We can't just talk about the word; we need a strategy

for it. Unforgiveness is spiritual bondage. It builds up a wall around your heart, protecting you from the outside world. I am not talking about protection from things we know may harm ourselves and our loved ones. I'm talking about missing the beautiful things in life that the Healer desires for us to enjoy for fear of being hurt again. I spent so much time trying to protect myself from the next Pulpit Predator I built a wall so high that I began missing out on the relationships that mattered most. Anytime I felt I was not in control of a situation, I would sabotage it. It was better for me to destroy it before it could hurt me. It cost me a lot of opportunities and almost my family. The wall had to be deconstructed brick by brick. It was painful. I hated it at first. Okay, to be honest, I still hate it, but the reward far outweighs the pain. Each brick had the name of a person or situation I had to face. It was emotional, and I was vulnerable, and I was mad as hell. God used and continues to use all of it.

Some chapters had me in a fetal position, emotional, as I saw things from the outside looking in for the first time. Sometimes, I was highly vulnerable as I shared my experiences without vomiting pain all over the pages. I needed to leave room for you to see every Target, not just me. I was mad that there were other Targets we may never know of. There is no need for there to be another.

Forgiveness starts with confession, but there must be a safe and healthy environment for that to take place. There needs to be an acknowledgment that manipulation, abuse,

PREDATOR IN THE PULPIT ~ 91

and deception have been committed. No Target feels safe if they feel unheard. Any incorrect theology must be addressed, any teaching that says the church leader is above reproach and should be obeyed has got to go, and any idolization of an individual must be redirected back to God. A plan of accountability and resolution should include the Target and Wounded when drafted.

The repair process is a long journey. Part of that journey must include education on Clergy Sexual Misconduct. The study conducted by Baylor University offers some great insight into preventing CSM. Prevention is crucial in dealing with any form of abuse.

Strategies for Preventing Clergy Sexual Misconduct For Religious Leaders and Those Who Supervise Them:

1. Religious leaders should not offer professional services beyond their qualifications. If they have not been educated as mental health professionals, they should not attempt to offer counseling or psychotherapy.

2. Religious leaders who have been prepared as mental health professionals should not offer mental health services (counseling or psychotherapy) to persons whom they also serve in the role of pastor, priest, rabbi, religious teacher, or supervisor.

3. Religious leaders should have accountability struc-

tures such as supervisors, peer groups, or congregational committees to whom they report on a regular
basis. They should share with this group the nature
of the relationships they are developing in the
congregation, particularly the development of close
friendships and family-like ties. The accountability
structure should also have direct access to congregants and assessments of the religious leader's
functioning.

4. Religious leaders should never use private information given to them by congregants for leaders' own
purposes.

For Congregations:

1. Educate members on the role of sexuality and
power in relationships, studying religious texts and
principles that relate to our sexuality and handling
the power we have (whether as parents, teachers, employers, supervisors, and leaders) and how a
community is responsible for its members who are
vulnerable to the misuse of power.

2. Educate members about the normalcy bias, the norm
of niceness, and the kinds of situations in which
we have experienced these disincentives to act and
appropriate responses.

3. Adopt written codes of ethics and clear role

expectations for leaders. Those expectations should include proscribing congregational leaders from serving in the dual role of professional counselor or therapist.

4. Conduct thorough reference checks on potential leaders, including persons in previous congregations not selected as references by the leader.

5. Provide accountability structures with regular reporting expectations.

As you can see, there is much to do in the repair. This may require outside interventions such as a licensed therapist trained in dealing with CSM, who could be available to deal with the emotional hurt of the Wounded. Whether or not the Wounded is open to receiving that help, it should still be available. Jesus AND therapy are okay. Remember, there is a stigma around Christians seeking mental health support. Their faith and prayer life are at times questioned. As a body of believers, we must address this stigma in the church before it is adequately addressed in our community.

The Target will also need a great deal of therapy. Therapists trained in CSM will be beneficial, but training in PTSD is mandatory. What the Target has gone through is a traumatic experience that can only be addressed by a licensed mental health professional. Faith-based counseling from another pastor or leader of the same congregation as the event should by no means be attempted. The Target will need support from family, friends, and congregation members. Blaming the Target will only delay the healing process.

The Partner needs the same level of therapy and education as the Wounded. Partners who assist in predatory behavior or CSM should seek professional behavioral therapy. They should resign from all leadership positions until healing has occurred. The congregation also needs to support the Partner. Support is not an acceptance of misbehavior or dismissal of accountability but aids in restoration.

All parties involved must be willing to engage in the process of repair. Let it be known that this is a process. There is no expiration date for when this is over, so exercising care, patience, grace, and love is essential. Neither the Partner, the Wounded, and especially the Target should feel rushed or pressured to "get over it" or forgive.

An oversight committee should be created if one has not already been established. If previously existing, a review from an outside agent should determine if committee members acted as the Partner by disregarding misconduct. When any form of abuse is reported or rumored, all allegations must be taken seriously and investigated regardless of the age of the Target. The committee should set in place regulations and policies that protect the congregants from any form of abuse. No pastoral staff or leadership should go without oversight. The church leader who can make all the decisions without accountability is dangerous.

During the repair process, the Wounded will still need the word of God presented just as it would before the event. The Pulpit Predator should not provide pastoral care, sermons, or teachings. The person on whom the responsibility falls should do so with love and care. The teachings should not be related to the event or with back-handed comments in support of the Pulpit Predator or blame for the Target. The focus should be repairing the Wounded's faith and eventual trust in leadership. Humble servant leadership is the best way to restore the Wounded. Servant leadership seeks to serve the Wounded's needs, not the leaders. Jesus was a servant leader:

"Jesus knew that the Father had given him authority over everything and that he had come from God and would return to God. So he got up from the table, took off his robe, wrapped a towel around his waist, and poured water into a basin. Then he began to wash the disciples' feet, drying them with the towel he had around him." **John 13:3-5 NLT**

All authority is a gift—a privilege to be taken seriously and diligently.

For the Predator:

A Pulpit Predator is not beyond the reach of God

and can be restored. To be restored, several things must be implemented. First and foremost, accountability. Accountability for a Pulpit Predator cannot happen without oversight. That is why an oversight committee or governing board should be in place. Pastors without oversight can quickly become Pulpit Predators, leaving the Target no place to report events or get help.

A Pulpit Predator should have godly counseling and professional therapy. Leaders are not superhuman, and doing ministry alone is never a good option. While accountability partners are good and should be required, it is not the same as counseling and therapy. A licensed therapist is equipped to deal with the mental health challenges of predatory behavior. It can also help deal with the weight of ministry. Leaders can be some of the most isolated members of a congregation, all while surrounded by people. They are expected to be perfect and please everyone at all times. Their time is expected to be at the beck and call of any issue regarding the church, at the expense of their families and themselves. Therapy can help them learn how to balance both ministry and personal life. Seeking therapy is not a sign of weakness but one of great strength.

No human is born a predator. It is a learned behavior. Unchecked pridefulness and imbalanced desires or an immoral compass lead to predatory behavior. Identifying the seed or root of the heart issue that led to predatory behavior is a step toward keeping it from happening again.

~ 13 ~

THE RESOURCES

■ RAINN: National Sexual Assault Hotline

https://www.rainn.org/resources

■ 988 Suicide and Crisis Hotline

https://988lifeline.org

■ SNAP: Survivors Network of the Abused by Priest

https://www.snapnetwork.org

■ Lewis + Llewelyn, LLP (Fighting Sexual Abuse)

https://sexualabuselawfirm.com/sexual-abuse/
church-clergy/

- Choosing Therapy

https://www.choosingtherapy.com/faith-based-coun-seling/

- Clergy Sexual Misconduct Information & Resources

https://clergysexualmisconduct.com/home

- The Hope of Survivors

http://www.thehopeofsurvivors.org

- FaithTrust Institute

https://www.faithtrustinstitute.org

- Not The Other Women

https://www.nottheotherwoman.com/informa-tion-and-resources

- Not In Our Church

https://www.notinourchurch.com

- AdvocateWeb

https://www.advocateweb.org/victim-resources-2/spiritual-resources/

Resources were made available to you, but I want you to know that I am here for you. You can send me an email or DM me on social media. I would love to hear your stories and your testimonies.

Contact Info: nikisha@warriorprincessnation.com
Facebook: facebook.com/warriorprincessnation
Instagram: @warriorprincessnation

Abba Father, it is my prayer that hearts are healed, minds are transformed, and You be glorified.

The Joy of the Lord is My Strength
Heather K Photography

Nikisha Sims is grateful for her unique gifts, and everything she does is accredited to her relationship with Yahweh and His love for people. She is married to the humorous Randy Sims, and they have two awesome adult children, Briana and Matthew. She is currently residing in Las Vegas, Nevada, but is a Northern California native. Nikisha is a Kingdom entrepreneur and visionary for Warrior Princess Nation and Hope City International. She is also an author, publisher, writing coach, podcaster, certified parent educator, speaker, and licensed minister.

With all of that said, Nikisha is simply passionate about helping others share their stories and understand their identity to grow into their calling and life purpose. The motto of her company is "Write great stories, live greater lives." That is what drives her passion to create a space for storytelling that brings about healing. You will often hear her say, "Everybody has a story, and every story matters."